THE PATRISTIC TREASURY

THE FIRST EPISTLE OF CLEMENT TO THE
CORINTHIANS
CLEMENT OF ROME

THE PATRISTIC TREASURY

THE FIRST EPISTLE OF CLEMENT TO THE
CORINTHIANS
CLEMENT OF ROME

Edited by
PHILIP SCHAFF
ALEXANDER ROBERTS, JAMES DONALD

cántaro
publications

cántaro
publications

cantaroinstitute.org

The First Epistle of Clement to the Corinthians
by Clement of Rome

Edited by Philip Schaff (1819-1893)
Alexander Roberts, D.D.
James Donaldson, LL.D.

Published by Cántaro Publications, a publishing imprint of the Cántaro Institute, Jordan Station, ON.

© 2022 by Cántaro Institute. All rights reserved. Except for brief quotations in critical publications or reviews, no part of this book may be reproduced in any manner without prior written consent from the publishers.

Book design by Steven R. Martins

Library & Archives Canada

ISBN 978-1-990771-01-9

Printed in the United States of America

TABLE OF CONTENTS

Series Preface ix

INTRODUCTORY NOTE 1

I　The Salutation 7

II　Praise Of The Corinthians 9

III　The Sad State Of The Corinthian Church 11

IV　Many Evils Have Already Flowed 13

V　No Less Evils Have Arisen 15

VI　Continuation: Several Other Martyrs 17

VII　An Exhortation To Repentance 19

VIII　Continuation Respecting Repentance 21

IX　Examples Of The Saints 23

X　Continuation Of The Above 25

XI　Continuation: Lot 27

XII　The Rewards Of Faith And Hospitality: Rahab 29

XIII　An Exhortation To Humility 31

XIV　We Should Obey God Rather Than The Authors Of Sedition 33

XV　We Must Adhere To Those Who Cultivate Peace 35

XVI　Christ As An Example Of Humility 37

XVII　The Saints As Examples Of Humility 39

XVIII　David As An Example Of Humility 41

XIX	Imitating These Examples, Let Us Seek After Peace	43
XX	The Peace And Harmony Of The Universe	45
XXI	Let Us Obey God, And Not The Authors Of Sedition	47
XXII	These Exhortations Are Confirmed By The Christian Faith	49
XXIII	Be Humble, And Believe That Christ Will Come Again	51
XXIV	God Continually Shows Us In Nature That There Will Be A Resurrection	53
XXV	The Phoenix An Emblem Of Our Resurrection	55
XXVI	We Shall Rise Again, Then, As The Scripture Also Testifies	57
XXVII	In The Hope Of The Resurrection, Let Us Cleave	59
XXVIII	God Sees All Things	61
XXIX	Let Us Also Draw Near To God In Purity Of Heart	63
XXX	Let Us Do Those Things That Please God	65
XXXI	Let Us See By What Means We May Obtain The Divine Blessing	67
XXXII	We Are Justified Not By Our Works, But By Faith	69
XXXIII	But Let Us Not Give Up The Practice Of Good Works And Love	71
XXXIV	Great Is The Reward Of Good Works With God	73

XXXV	Immense Is This Reward	75
XXXVI	All Blessings Are Given To Us Through Christ	77
XXXVII	Christ Is Our Leader And We His Soldiers	79
XXXVIII	Let The Members Of The Church Submit Themselves	81
XXXIX	There Is No Reason For Self-Conceit	83
XL	Let Us Preserve In The Church The Order Appointed By God	85
XLI	Continuation of the Same Subject	87
XLII	The Order Of Ministers In The Church	89
XLIII	Moses Of Old Stilled The Contention Which Arose Concerning The Priestly Dignity	91
XLIV	The Ordinances Of The Apostles	93
XLV	It Is The Part Of The Wicked To Vex The Righteous	95
XLVI	Let Us Cleave To The Righteous	97
XLVII	Your Recent Discord Is Worse Than The Former Which Took Place In The Times Of Paul	99
XLVIII	Let Us Return To The Practice Of Brotherly Love	101
XLIX	The Praise Of Love	103
L	Let Us Pray To Be Thought Worthy Of Love	105
LI	Let The Partakers In Strife Acknowledge Their Sins	107
LII	Such A Confession Is Pleasing To God	109

LIII	The Love Of Moses Towards His People	111
LIV	He Who Is Full Of Love Will Incur Every Loss That Peace May Be Restored To The Church	113
LV	Examples Of Such Love	115
LVI	Let Us Admonish And Correct One Another	117
LVII	Let The Authors Of Sedition Submit Themselves	119
LVIII	Blessings Sought For All That Call Upon God	121
LIX	The Corinthians Are Exhorted Speedily To Send Back Word That Peace Has Been Restored	123

SERIES PREFACE

My initial introduction to the Patristics—the writings of the early Church Fathers—came through Dr. David Robinson, then serving as an adjunct professor of Church History at Tyndale University College & Seminary. Dr. Robinson, now adjunct professor of Biblical Studies and Theology at Tyndale, contributed the introduction and commentary notes to Francis X. Gumerlock's translation of Tyconius' works in *The Fathers of the Church: Tyconius of Carthage*. He also served as co-pastor with Joe Boot at Westminster Chapel in Toronto, Ontario, where my wife and I worshiped prior to relocating to the Niagara region. Dr. Robinson currently serves as Lead Pastor of Westminster Chapel.

I remember attending his regular Wednesday evening gatherings, during which he guided us through the Patristics—each week highlighting a different figure and weaving their insights into his Sunday sermons. Among the many luminaries he presented, his treatment of St. Athanasius left the deepest impression on me. Until then, the Church Fathers had been largely absent from my thinking and practice, yet by God's providence I was led to discover the rich treasury of the Patristics. Although I have only begun to engage the works of the ante-Nicene, Nicene, and post-Nicene Fathers—not as a dedicated scholar but as an eager student of church history—I have been profoundly edified and encouraged. In the sweep of the church's early centuries (and indeed beyond) we behold God's power and sovereignty in preserving His church against both internal false teachers and external existential threats. The church does not endure because of its own strength but in spite of its weaknesses, bearing witness and bringing glory to the God who saves and sustains. As *The Epistle Concerning the Mar-*

tyrdom of Polycarp records, "we, to whom it was given to witness it, beheld a great miracle, and have been preserved that we might report to others what then took place."

As we read the Patristics, we will at times be struck with awe at the profundity of their wisdom and insight, and at other times find ourselves bewildered as we wrestle to understand certain passages. In short, the writings of the Church Fathers are a "mixed bag"; yet this does not diminish their value. They are "mixed" in part because the soundness of doctrine varies among authors and texts, and also because some emphases are deeply contextual—directly relevant to the controversies of their own day but less immediately relatable to ours—while still illuminating the church's history and its engagement with culture. We should remember that the Fathers belonged to the early, or "primitive," church—not in the quality of their faith, but in the degree of their doctrinal development—and that we, with the benefit of centuries of theological reflection, now possess a far greater treasury of Christian wisdom. This perspective should inform but not negate our reading, for the Holy Spirit was at work through the Patristics, even though their writings themselves are not inspired. Indeed, they remain richly edifying for Christian life and thought today. Moreover, the Fathers consistently ground their arguments in Scripture, citing it extensively and acknowledging its supreme authority. We, therefore, ought to read the Patristics through this corrective and authoritative lens, recognizing that only the divinely inspired Scriptures provide the definitive interpretation of created reality.

It is therefore the pleasure and privilege of the Cántaro Institute to republish select works of the Church Fathers—texts that have long been out of print and reverted to the public domain—in a new series entitled *The Patristic Treasury*. Our hope is that this collection will prove as edifying, encouraging, and enlightening to today's readers as it has been to us. While certain aspects of the Fathers' writings may no longer directly apply in every context, much of their work continues to shed light on the enduring internal and external challenges faced by the church. Within these texts we encounter a treasury of wisdom and guidance that has strengthened the church for two millennia and has not ceased to do so. As the scholar Michael A. G. Haykin observes, "Many of our Evangelical forebears read the Fathers, and that reading enriched their lives and thought. We need to do the same to help us meet some of the great challenges of our day."[1]

Dei gratia,

Steven R. Martins
Founding Director
Cántaro Institute

---

1. Justin Taylor, "Reading the Church Fathers: A Beginner's Guide", *The Gospel Coalition*. Accessed March 9, 2022, https://www.thegospelcoalition.org/blogs/justin-taylor/reading-the-church-fathers-a-beginners-guide/.; See Michael A.G. Haykin, *Rediscovering the Church Fathers: Who They Were and How They Shaped the Church* (Wheaton, IL.: Crossway, 2011).

THE FIRST EPISTLE OF CLEMENT
TO THE CORINTHIANS

CLEMENT OF ROME

Edited by Philip Schaff (1819-1893)
Alexander Roberts, D.D.
James Donaldson, LL.D.

INTRODUCTORY NOTE TO THE FIRST EPISTLE OF CLEMENT TO THE CORINTHIANS

[AD 30-100] Clement was probably a Gentile and a Roman. He seems to have been at Philippi with St. Paul (AD 57) when that first-born of the Western churches was passing through great trials of faith. There, with holy women and others, he ministered to the apostle and to the saints. As this city was a Roman colony, we need not inquire how a Roman happened to be there. He was possibly in some public service, and it is not improbable that he had visited Corinth in those days. From the apostle, and his companion, St. Luke, he had no doubt learned the use of the Septuagint, in which his knowledge of the Greek tongue soon rendered him an adept. His copy of that version, however, does not always agree with the Received Text, as the reader will perceive.

A co-presbyter with Linus and Cletus, he succeeded them in the government of the Roman Church. I have reluctantly adopted the opinion that his Epistle was written near the close of his life, and not just after the persecution of Nero. It is not improbable that Linus and Cletus both perished in that fiery trial, and that Clement's immediate succession to their work and place occasions the chronological difficulties of the period. After the death of the apostles, for the Roman imprisonment and martyrdom of St. Peter seem historical, Clement was the natural representative of St. Paul, and even of his companion, the "apostle of the circumcision"; and naturally he wrote the Epistle in the name of the local church, when brethren looked to them for advice. St. John, no doubt, was still surviving at Patmos or in Ephesus; but the Philippians, whose intercourse with Rome is attested by the visit of Epaphroditus, looked naturally to the surviving friends of their great founder;

1

nor was the aged apostle in the East equally accessible. All roads pointed towards the Imperial City, and started from its *Milliarium Aureum*. But, though Clement doubtless wrote the letter, he conceals his own name, and puts forth the brethren, who seem to have met in council, and sent a brotherly delegation (Chap. LIX). The entire absence of the spirit of Diotrephes (3 John 9), and the close accordance of the Epistle, in humility and meekness, with that of St. Peter (1 Peter 5:1-5), are noteworthy features. The whole will be found animated with the loving and faithful spirit of St. Paul's dear Philippians, among whom the writer had learned the Gospel.

Clement fell asleep, probably soon after he dispatched his letter. It is the legacy of one who reflects the apostolic age in all the beauty and evangelical truth which were the first-fruits of the Spirit's presence with the Church. He shares with others the aureole of glory attributed by St. Paul (Philippians 4:3), "His name is in the Book of Life."

The following is the Introductory Notice of the original editors and translators, Drs. Roberts and Donaldson:

The first Epistle, bearing the name of Clement, has been preserved to us in a single manuscript only at the date of this writing. Though very frequently referred to by ancient Christian writers, it remained unknown to the scholars of Western Europe until happily discovered in the Alexandrian manuscript. This ms. of the Sacred Scriptures (known and generally referred to as Codex A) was presented in 1628 by Cyril, Patriarch of Constantinople, to Charles I., and is now preserved in the British Museum. Subjoined to the books of the New Testament contained in it, there are two writings described as the Epistles of one Clement. Of these, that now before us is the first. It is tolerably perfect, but there are many slight *lacunae*, or gaps, in the ms., and one whole leaf is supposed to have been lost towards the close. These *lacunae*, however, so numerous in some chapters, do not generally extend beyond a word or syllable, and can for the most part be easily supplied.

Who the Clement was to whom these writings are ascribed, cannot with absolute certainty be determined. The general opinion is, that he is the same as the person of that name referred to by St. Paul (Philippians 4:3). The writings themselves contain no statement as to their author. The first, and by far the longer of them, simply purports to have been written in the name of the Church at Rome to the Church at Corinth. But in the catalogue of contents prefixed to the ms. they are both plainly attributed to one Clement; and the judgment of most scholars is, that, in regard to the first Epistle at least, this statement is correct, and that it is to be regarded as an authentic production of the friend and fellow-worker of St. Paul. This belief may be traced to an early period in the history of the Church. It is found in the writings of Eusebius (Hist. Eccl., iii. 15), of Origen (Comm. in Joan., i. 29), and others. The internal evidence also tends to support this opinion. The doctrine, style, and manner of thought are all in accordance with it; so that, although, as has been said, positive certainty cannot be reached on the subject, we may with great probability conclude that we have in this Epistle a composition of that Clement who is known to us from Scripture as having been an associate of the great apostle.

The date of this Epistle has been the subject of considerable controversy. It is clear from the writing itself that it was composed soon after some persecution (chap. 1) which the Roman Church had endured; and the only question is, whether we are to fix upon the persecution under Nero or Domitian. If the former, the date will be about the youar 68; if the latter, we must place it towards the close of the first century or the beginning of the second. We possess no external aid to the settlement of this question. The lists of early Roman bishops are in hopeless confusion, some making Clement the immediate successor of St. Peter, others placing Linus, and others still Linus and Anacletus, between him and the apostle. The internal evidence, again, leaves the matter doubtful, though it has been strongly pressed on both sides. The probability seems, on the whole, to be in favour of the Domitian period, so that the Epistle may be dated about AD 97.

This Epistle was held in very great esteem by the early Church. The account given of it by Eusebius (Hist. Eccl., iii. 16) is as follows:

> There is one acknowledged Epistle of this Clement (whom he has just identified with the friend of St. Paul), great and admirable, which he wrote in the name of the Church of Rome to the Church at Corinth, sedition having then arisen in the latter Church. We are aware that this Epistle has been publicly read in very many churches both in old times, and also in our own day.

The Epistle before us thus appears to have been read in numerous churches, as being almost on a level with the canonical writings. And its place in the Alexandrian ms., immediately after the inspired books, is in harmony with the position thus assigned it in the primitive Church. There does indeed appear a great difference between it and the inspired writings in many respects, such as the fanciful use sometimes made of Old-Testament statements, the fabulous stories which are accepted by its author, and the general diffuseness and feebleness of style by which it is distinguished. But the high tone of evangelical truth which pervades it, the simple and earnest appeals which it makes to the heart and conscience, and the anxiety which its writer so constantly shows to promote the best interests of the Church of Christ, still impart an undying charm to this precious relic of later apostolic times.[1]

EDINBURGH, 1867

---

1. A sufficient guide to the recent literature of the Clementine mss. and discoveries may be found in *The Princeton Review*, 1877, p. 325, also in Bishop Wordsworth's succinct but learned *Church History to the Council of Nicaea*, p. 84. The invaluable edition of the *Patres Apostolici*, by Jacobson (Oxford, 1840), with a critical text and rich prolegomena and annotations, cannot be dispensed with by any Patristic inquirer. A.C.C.

CHAPTER I

The Salutation: Praise Of The Corinthians Before The Breaking Forth Of Schism Among Them

The Church of God which sojourns at Rome, to the Church of God sojourning at Corinth, to them that are called and sanctified by the will of God, through our Lord Jesus Christ: Grace unto you, and peace, from Almighty God through Jesus Christ, be multiplied.

Owing, dear brethren, to the sudden and successive calamitous events which have happened to ourselves, we feel that we have been somewhat tardy in turning our attention to the points respecting which you consulted us;[1] and especially to that shameful and detestable sedition, utterly abhorrent to the elect of God, which a few rash and self-confident persons have kindled to such a pitch of frenzy, that your venerable and illustrious name, worthy to be universally loved, has suffered grievous injury.[2] For whoever dwelt even for a short time among you, and did not find your faith to be as fruitful of virtue as it was firmly established?[3] Who did not admire the sobriety and moderation of your godliness in Christ? Who did not proclaim the magnificence of your habitual hospitality? And who did not rejoice over your perfect and well-grounded knowledge? For you did all things without respect of persons, and walked in the commandments of God, being obedient to those

---

1. Note the fact that the Corinthians asked this of their brethren, the personal friends of their apostle St. Paul. Clement's own name does not appear in this Epistle.
2. Literally, "is greatly blasphemed."
3. Literally, "did not prove your all-virtuous and firm faith."

who had the rule over you, and giving all fitting honour to the presbyters among you. You enjoined young men to be of a sober and serious mind; you instructed your wives to do all things with a blameless, becoming, and pure conscience, loving their husbands as in duty bound; and you taught them that, living in the rule of obedience, they should manage their household affairs becomingly, and be in every respect marked by discretion.

CHAPTER II

Praise Of The Corinthians Continued

MOREOVER, YOU WERE ALL distinguished by humility, and were in no respect puffed up with pride, but yielded obedience rather than extorted it,[1] and were more willing to give than to receive.[2] Content with the provision which God had made for you, and carefully attending to His words, you were inwardly filled[3] with His doctrine, and His sufferings were before your eyous. Thus a profound and abundant peace was given to you all, and you had an insatiable desire for doing good, while a full outpouring of the Holy Spirit was upon you all. Full of holy designs, you did, with true earnestness of mind and a godly confidence, stretch forth your hands to God Almighty, beseeching Him to be merciful unto you, if you had been guilty of any involuntary transgression. Day and night you were anxious for the whole brotherhood,[4] that the number of God›s elect might be saved with mercy and a good conscience.[5] You were sincere and uncorrupted, and forgetful of injuries between one *another*. Every kind of faction and schism was abominable in your sight. You mourned over the transgressions of your neighbours: their deficiencies you deemed your own.

1. Eph. 5:21; 1 Pet. 5:5
2. Acts 20:35
3. Literally, "you embraced it in your bowels." [Concerning the complaints of Photius (ninth century) against Clement, see Bull's *Defensio Fidei Nicaenae, Works*, vol. v. p. 132.]
4. 1 Pet. 2:17
5. So, in the ms., but many have suspected that the text is here corrupt. Perhaps the best emendation is that which substitutes συναισθήσεως, "compassion" for συνειδήσεως, "conscience."

You never grudged any act of kindness, being "ready to every good work."⁶ Adorned by a thoroughly virtuous and religious life, you did all things in the fear of God. The commandments and ordinances of the Lord were written upon the tablets of your hearts.⁷

---

6. Tit. 3:1
7. Prov. 7:3

CHAPTER III

The Sad State Of The Corinthian Church After Sedition Arose In It From Envy And Emulation

EVERY KIND OF HONOUR and happiness[1] was bestowed upon you, and then was fulfilled that which is written, "My beloved did eat and drink, and was enlarged and became fat, and kicked."[2] Hence flowed emulation and envy, strife and sedition, persecution and disorder, war and captivity. So the worthless rose up against the honoured, those of no reputation against such as were renowned, the foolish against the wise, the young against those advanced in years. For this reason righteousness and peace are now far departed from you, inasmuch as everyone abandons the fear of God, and is become blind in His faith,[3] neither walks in the ordinances of His appointment, nor acts a part becoming a Christian,[4] but walks after his own wicked lusts, resuming the practice of an unrighteous and ungodly envy, by which death itself entered into the world.[5]

---

1. Literally, "enlargement" ".
2. Deut. 32:15
3. It seems necessary to refer αὐτοῦ to God, in opposition to the translation given by Abp. Wake and others.
4. Literally, "Christ;" comp. 2 Cor. 1:21, Eph. 4:20
5. Wisdom 2:24.

CHAPTER IV

Many Evils Have Already Flowed From This Source In Ancient Times

For thus it is written:

> And it came to pass after certain days, that Cain brought of the fruits of the earth a sacrifice unto God; and Abel also brought of the firstlings of his sheep, and of the fat thereof. And God had respect to Abel and to his offerings, but Cain and his sacrifices He did not regard. And Cain was deeply grieved, and his countenance fell. And God said to Cain, Why art thou grieved, and why is thy countenance fallen? If thou offerest rightly, but dost not divide rightly, hast thou not sinned? Be at peace: thine offering returns to thyself, and thou shalt again possess it. And Cain said to Abel his brother, Let us go into the field. And it came to pass, while they were in the field, that Cain rose up against Abel his brother, and slew him.[1]

You see, brethren, how envy and jealousy led to the murder of a brother. Through envy, also, our father Jacob fled from the face of Esau his brother.[2] Envy made Joseph be persecuted unto death, and to come into bondage.[3] Envy compelled Moses to flee from the face of Pharaoh king of Egypt, when he heard these

---

1. Gen. 4:3–8. The writer here, as always, follows the reading of the Septuagint, which in this passage both alters and adds to the Hebrew text. We have given the rendering approved by the best critics; but some prefer to translate, as in our English version, "unto thee shall be his desire, and thou shalt rule over him." See, for an ancient explanation of the passage, Irenæus, *Adv. Hær.*, 4:18, 3.
2. Gen. 27:41, etc.
3. Gen. 37

words from his fellow-countryman, "Who made thee a judge or a ruler over us? wilt thou kill me, as thou didst kill the Egyptian yesterday?"[4] On account of envy, Aaron and Miriam had to make their abode without the camp.[5] Envy brought down Dathan and Abiram alive to Hades, through the sedition which they excited against God's servant Moses.[6] Through envy, David underwent the hatred not only of foreigners, but was also persecuted by Saul king of Israel.[7]

---

4. Exod. 2:14.
5. Num. 12:14, 15. [In our copies of the Septuagint this is not affirmed of Aaron.]
6. Num. 26:33.
7. 1 Kings xviii. 8, etc.

CHAPTER V

No Less Evils Have Arisen From The Same Source In The Most Recent Times: The Martyrdom Of Peter And Paul

BUT NOT TO DWELL UPON ancient examples, let us come to the most recent spiritual heroes.[1] Let us take the noble examples furnished in our own generation. Through envy and jealousy, the greatest and most righteous pillars [of the Church] have been persecuted and put to death.[2] Let us set before our eyes the illustrious apostles.[3] Peter, through unrighteous envy, endured not one or two, but numerous labours and when he had at length suffered martyrdom, departed to the place of glory due to him. Owing to envy, Paul also obtained the reward of patient endurance, after being seven times thrown into captivity,[4] compelled[5] to flee, and stoned. After preaching both in the East and West, he gained the illustrious reputation due to his faith, having taught righteousness to the whole world, and come to the extreme limit of the

---

1. Literally, "those who have been athletes."
2. Some fill up the lacuna here found in the ms. so as to read, "have come to a grievous death."
3. Literally, "good." [The martyrdom of St. Peter is all that is thus connected with his arrival in Rome. His numerous labours were restricted to the Circumcision.]
4. *Seven* imprisonments of St. Paul are not referred to in Scripture.
5. Archbishop Wake here reads "scourged." We have followed the most recent critics in filling up the numerous *lacunæ* in this chapter.

West,⁶ and suffered martyrdom under the prefects.⁷ Thus was he removed from the world, and went into the holy place, having proved himself a striking example of patience.

---

6. Some think *Rome*, others *Spain*, and others even *Britain*, to be here referred to.
7. That is, under Tigellinus and Sabinus, in the last year of the Emperor Nero; but some think Helius and Polycletus are referred to; and others, both here and in the preceding sentence, regard the words as denoting simply the *witness* borne by Peter and Paul to the truth of the gospel before the rulers of the earth.

CHAPTER VI

Continuation: Several Other Martyrs

To THESE MEN who spent their lives in the practice of holiness, there is to be added a great multitude of the elect, who, having through envy endured many indignities and tortures, furnished us with a most excellent example. Through envy, those women, the Danaids[1] and Dircae, being persecuted, after they had suffered terrible and unspeakable torments, finished the course of their faith with steadfastness,[2] and though weak in body, received a noble reward. Envy has alienated wives from their husbands, and changed that saying of our father Adam, "This is now bone of my bones, and flesh of my flesh."[3] Envy and strife have overthrown great cities and rooted up mighty nations.

---

1. Some suppose these to have been the names of two eminent female martyrs under Nero; others regard the clause as an interpolation. [Many ingenious conjectures might be cited; but see Jacobson's valuable note, *Patres Apostol.*, vol. i. p. 30.]
2. Literally, "have reached to the steadfast course of faith."
3. Gen. 2:23

CHAPTER VII

An Exhortation To Repentance

THESE THINGS, BELOVED, we write unto you, not merely to admonish you of your duty, but also to remind ourselves. For we are struggling on the same arena, and the same conflict is assigned to both of us. Wherefore let us give up vain and fruitless cares, and approach to the glorious and venerable rule of our holy calling. Let us attend to what is good, pleasing, and acceptable in the sight of Him who formed us. Let us look steadfastly to the blood of Christ, and see how precious that blood is to God,[1] which, having been shed for our salvation, has set the grace of repentance before the whole world. Let us turn to every age that has passed, and learn that, from generation to generation, the Lord has granted a place of repentance to all such as would be converted unto Him. Noah preached repentance, and as many as listened to him were saved.[2] Jonah proclaimed destruction to the Ninevites;[3] but they, repenting of their sins, propitiated God by prayer, and obtained salvation, although they were aliens [to the covenant] of God.

---

1. Some insert "Father."
2. Gen. 7; 1 Pet. 3:20; 2 Pet. 2:5.
3. Jon. 3

CHAPTER VIII

Continuation Respecting Repentance

THE MINISTERS OF THE GRACE of God have, by the Holy Spirit, spoken of repentance; and the Lord of all things has himself declared with an oath regarding it, "As I live, saith the Lord, I desire not the death of the sinner, but rather his repentance";[1] adding, moreover, this gracious declaration:

> Repent O house of Israel, of your iniquity.[2] Say to the children of My people, Though your sins reach from earth to heaven, I and though they be redder[3] than scarlet, and blacker than sackcloth, yet if you turn to Me with your whole heart, and say, Father! I will listen to you, as to a holy[4] people.

And in another place He speaks thus:

> Wash ye, and become clean; put away the wickedness of your souls from before mine eyes; cease from your evil ways, and learn to do well; seek out judgment, deliver the oppressed, judge the fatherless, and see that justice is done to the widow; and come, and let us reason together. He declares, Though your sins be like crimson, I will make them white as snow; though they be like scarlet, I will whiten them like wool. And if you be willing and obey Me, you shall eat the good of the land; but if you refuse, and will not hearken unto Me, the sword shall devour ye, for the mouth of the Lord hath spoken

---

1. Ezek. 33:11
2. Ezek. 18:30
3. Comp. Isa. 1:18
4. These words are not found in Scripture, though they are quoted again by Clem. Alex. (*Pædag.*, i. 10) as from Ezekiel.

these things."⁵

Desiring, therefore, that all His beloved should be partakers of repentance, He has, by His almighty will, established [these declarations].

---
5. Isa. 1:16-20

Chapter IX
Examples Of The Saints

WHEREFORE, LET US YIELD obedience to His excellent and glorious will; and imploring His mercy and loving-kindness, while we forsake all fruitless labours,[1] and strife, and envy, which leads to death, let us turn and have recourse to His compassions. Let us steadfastly contemplate those who have perfectly ministered to His excellent glory. Let us take (for instance) Enoch, who, being found righteous in obedience, was translated, and death was never known to happen to him.[2] Noah, being found faithful, preached regeneration to the world through his ministry; and the Lord saved by him the animals which, with one accord, entered into the ark.

---

1. Some read ματαιολογίαν, "vain talk."
2. Gen. 5:24; Heb. 11:5. Literally, "and his death was not found."

CHAPTER X

Continuation Of The Above

Abraham, styled "the friend,"[1] was found faithful, inasmuch as he rendered obedience to the words of God. He, in the exercise of obedience, went out from his own country, and from his kindred, and from his father›s house, in order that, by forsaking a small territory, and a weak family, and an insignificant house, he might inherit the promises of God. For God said to him,

> Get thee out from thy country, and from thy kindred, and from thy father's house, into the land which I shall show thee. And I will make thee a great nation, and will bless thee, and make thy name great, and thou shall be blessed. And I will bless them that bless thee, and curse them that curse thee; and in thee shall all the families of the earth be blessed.[2]

And again, on his departing from Lot, God said to him.

> Lift up thine eyes, and look from the place where thou now art, northward, and southward, and eastward, and westward; for all the land which thou seest, to thee will I give it, and to thy seed for ever. And I will make thy seed as the dust of the earth, [so that] if a man can number the dust of the earth, then shall thy seed also be numbered.[3]

And again [the Scripture] saith, "God brought forth Abram, and spake unto him, Look up now to heaven, and count the stars if thou be able to number them; so shall thy seed be. And Abram

---

1. Isa. 41:8; 2 Chron. 20:7; Judith 8:19; Jas. 2:23
2. Gen. 12:1-3
3. Gen. 13:14-16

believed God, and it was counted to him for righteousness."[4] On account of his faith and hospitality, a son was given him in his old age; and in the exercise of obedience, he offered him as a sacrifice to God on one of the mountains which He showed him.[5]

---

4. Gen. 15:5, 6; Rom. 4:3
5. Gen. 21:22; Heb. 11:17

CHAPTER XI
Continuation: Lot

ON ACCOUNT OF HIS HOSPITALITY and godliness, Lot was saved out of Sodom when all the country round was punished by means of fire and brimstone, the Lord thus making it manifest that He does not forsake those that hope in Him, but gives up such as depart from Him to punishment and torture.[1] For Lot›s wife, who went forth with him, being of a different mind from himself and not continuing in agreement with him [as to the command which had been given them], was made an example of, so as to be a pillar of salt unto this day.[2] This was done that all might know that those who are of a double mind, and who distrust the power of God, bring down judgment on themselves[3] and become a sign to all succeeding generations.

---

1. Gen. 19; comp. 2 Pet. 2:6-9
2. So Joseph., *Antiq.*, i. 11, 4; Irenæus, *Adv. Hær.*, iv. 31.
3. Literally, "become a judgment and sign."

CHAPTER XII

The Rewards Of Faith And Hospitality: Rahab

ON ACCOUNT OF HER FAITH and hospitality, Rahab the harlot was saved. For when spies were sent by Joshua, the son of Nun, to Jericho, the king of the country ascertained that they were come to spy out their land, and sent men to seize them, in order that, when taken, they might be put to death. But the hospitable Rahab receiving them, concealed them on the roof of her house under some stalks of flax. And when the men sent by the king arrived and said "There came men unto thee who are to spy out our land; bring them forth, for so the king commands," she answered them, "The two men whom you seek came unto me, but quickly departed again and are gone," thus not discovering the spies to them. Then she said to the men, "I know assuredly that the Lord your God hath given you this city, for the fear and dread of you have fallen on its inhabitants. When therefore you shall have taken it, keep you me and the house of my father in safety." And they said to her, "It shall be as thou hast spoken to us. As soon, therefore, as thou knowest that we are at hand, thou shall gather all thy family under thy roof, and they shall be preserved, but all that. are found outside of thy dwelling shall perish."[1] Moreover, they gave her a sign to this effect, that she should hang forth from her house a scarlet thread. And thus they made it manifest that redemption should flow through the blood of the Lord to all them that believe and hope in God.[2] You see, beloved, that there was not only faith,

---

1. Josh. 2; Heb. 11:31
2. Others of the Fathers adopt the same allegorical interpretation, e.g., Justin Mar., *Dial. c. Tryph.*, n. 111; Irenæus, *Adv. Hær.*, iv. 20. [The whole matter of symbolism under the

but prophecy, in this woman.

---

law must be more thoroughly studied if we would account for such strong language as is here applied to a poetical or rhetorical figure.]

CHAPTER XIII
An Exhortation To Humility

Let us therefore, brethren, be of humble mind, laying aside all haughtiness, and pride, and foolishness, and angry feelings; and let us act according to that which is written (for the Holy Spirit saith, "Let not the wise man glory in his wisdom, neither let the mighty man glory in his might, neither let the rich man glory in his riches; but let him that glorieth glory in the Lord, in diligently seeking Him, and doing judgment and righteousness"[1]), being especially mindful of the words of the Lord Jesus which He spake, teaching us meekness and long-suffering. For thus He spoke:

> Be you merciful, that you may obtain mercy; forgive, that it may be forgiven to you; as you do, so shall it be done unto you; as you judge, so shall you be judged; as you are kind, so shall kindness be shown to you; with what measure you mete, with the same it shall be measured to you.[2]

By this precept and by these rules let us establish ourselves, that we walk with all humility in obedience to His holy words. For the holy word saith, "On whom shall I look, but on him that is meek and peaceable, and that trembleth at My words?"[3]

---

1. Jer. 9:23, 24; 1 Cor. 1:31; 2 Cor. 10:17
2. Comp. Matt. 6:12-15, Matt. 7:2; Luke 6:36-38
3. Isa. 66:2

CHAPTER XIV

We Should Obey God Rather Than The Authors Of Sedition

It is right and holy therefore, men and brethren, rather to obey God than to follow those who, through pride and sedition, have become the leaders of a detestable emulation. For we shall incur no slight injury, but rather great danger, if we rashly yield ourselves to the inclinations of men who aim at exciting strife and tumults, so as to draw us away from what is good. Let us be kind one to another after the pattern of the tender mercy and benignity of our Creator. For it is written, "The kind-hearted shall inhabit the land, and the guiltless shall be left upon it, but transgressors shall be destroyed from off the face of it."[1] And again [the Scripture] saith, "I saw the ungodly highly exalted, and lifted up like the cedars of Lebanon: I passed by, and, behold, he was not; and I diligently sought his place, and could not find it. Preserve innocence, and look on equity: for there shall be a remnant to the peaceful man."[2]

---

1. Prov. 2:21-22.
2. Ps. 37:35-37. "Remnant" probably refers either to the memory or posterity of the righteous.

CHAPTER XV

We Must Adhere To Those Who Cultivate Peace, Not To Those Who Merely Pretend To Do So

LET US CLEAVE, therefore, to those who cultivate peace with godliness, and not to those who hypocritically profess to desire it. For [the Scripture] saith in a certain place, "This people honoureth Me with their lips, but their heart is far from Me."[1] And again: "They bless with their mouth, but curse with their heart."[2] And again it saith, "They loved Him with their mouth, and lied to Him with their tongue; but their heart was not right with Him, neither were they faithful in His covenant."[3] "Let the deceitful lips become silent,"[4] [and "let the Lord destroy all the lying lips,[5]] and the boastful tongue of those who have said, Let us magnify our tongue; our lips are our own; who is lord over us? For the oppression of the poor, and for the sighing of the needy, will I now arise, saith the Lord: I will place him in safety; I will deal confidently with him."[6]

---

1. Isa. 29:13; Matt. 15:8; Mark 7:6
2. Ps. 62:4
3. Ps. 78:36, 37
4. Ps. 31:18
5. These words within brackets are not found in the ms., but have been inserted from the Septuagint by most editors.
6. Ps. 12:3-5.

CHAPTER XVI

Christ As An Example Of Humility

FOR CHRIST IS OF THOSE who are humble-minded, and not of those who exalt themselves over His flock. Our Lord Jesus Christ, the Sceptre of the majesty of God, did not come in the pomp of pride or arrogance, although He might have done so, but in a lowly condition, as the Holy Spirit had declared regarding Him. For He says,

> Lord, who hath believed our report, and to whom is the arm of the Lord revealed? We have declared [our message] in His presence: He is, as it were, a child, and like a root in thirsty ground; He has no form nor glory, yea, we saw Him, and He had no form nor comeliness; but His form was without eminence, yea, deficient in comparison with the [ordinary] form of men. He is a man exposed to stripes and suffering, acquainted with the endurance of grief: for His countenance was turned away; He was despised, and not esteemed. He bears our iniquities, and is in sorrow for our sakes; yet we supposed that [on His own account] He was exposed to labour, and stripes, and affliction. But He was wounded for our transgressions, and bruised for our iniquities. The chastisement of our peace was upon Him, and by His stripes we were healed. All we, like sheep, have gone astray; [every] man has wandered in his own way; and the Lord has delivered Him up for our sins, while He in the midst of His sufferings openeth not His mouth. He was brought as a sheep to the slaughter, and as a lamb before her shearer is dumb, so He openeth not His mouth. In His humiliation His judgment was taken away; who shall declare His generation? for His life is taken from the earth. For the transgressions of my people was He brought down to death. And I will give the wicked for His sepulchre, and the rich for His

death,[1] because He did no iniquity, neither was guile found in His mouth. And the Lord is pleased to purify Him by stripes.[2] If you make[3] an offering for sin, your soul shall see a long-lived seed. And the Lord is pleased to relieve Him of the affliction of His soul, to show Him light, and to form Him with understanding,[4] to justify the Just One who ministereth well to many; and the Himself shall carry their sins. On this account He shall inherit many, and shall divide the spoil of the strong; because His soul was delivered to death, and He was reckoned among the transgressors, and He bare the sins of many, and for their sins was He delivered.[5]

And again He saith, "I am a worm, and no man; a reproach of men, and despised of the people. All that see Me have derided Me; they have spoken with their lips; they have wagged their head, [saying] He hoped in God, let Him deliver Him, let Him save Him, since He delighteth in Him."[6] You see, beloved, what is the example which has been given us; for if the Lord thus humbled Himself, what shall we do who have through Him come under the yoke of His grace?

---

1. The Latin of Cotelerius, adopted by Hefele and Dressel, translates this clause as follows: "I will set free the wicked on account of His sepulchre, and the rich on account of His death."
2. The reading of the ms. is τῆς πληγῆς, "purify, or free, Him from stripes." We have adopted the emendation of Junius.
3. Wotton reads, "If He make."
4. Or, "*fill* Him with understanding," if πλῆσαι should be read instead of πλάσαι, as Grabe suggests.
5. Isa. 53. The reader will observe how often the text of the Septuagint, here quoted, differs from the Hebrew as represented by our authorized English version.
6. Ps. 22:6-8.

CHAPTER XVII

The Saints As Examples of Humility

Let us be imitators also of those who in goat-skins and sheep-skins[1] went about proclaiming the coming of Christ; I mean Elijah, Elisha, and Ezekiel among the prophets, with those others to whom a like testimony is borne [in Scripture]. Abraham was specially honoured, and was called the friend of God; yet he, earnestly regarding the glory of God, humbly declared, "I am but dust and ashes."[2] Moreover, it is thus written of Job, "Job was a righteous man, and blameless, truthful, God-fearing, and one that kept himself from all evil."[3] But bringing an accusation against himself, he said, "No man is free from defilement, even if his life be but of one day."[4] Moses was called faithful in all God›s house;[5] and through his instrumentality, God punished Egypt[6] with plagues and tortures. Yet he, though thus greatly honoured, did not adopt lofty language, but said, when the divine oracle came to him out of the bush, "Who am I, that Thou sendest me? I am a man of a feeble voice and a slow tongue."[7] And again he said, "I am but as the smoke of a pot."[8]

---

1. Heb. 11:37
2. Gen. 18:27
3. Job 1:1
4. Job 14:4, 5. [Septuagint.]
5. Num. 12:7; Heb. 3:2
6. Some fill up the *lacuna* which here occurs in the ms. by "Israel."
7. Exod. 3:11, Exod. 4:10.
8. This is not found in Scripture. [They were probably in Clement's version. Comp. Ps. 119:83.]

CHAPTER XVIII

David As An Example of Humility

BUT WHAT SHALL WE SAY concerning David, to whom such testimony was borne, and of whom[1] God said, "I have found a man after Mine own heart, David the son of Jesse; and in everlasting mercy have I anointed him?"[2] Yet this very man saith to God,

> Have mercy on me, O Lord, according to Thy great mercy; and according to the multitude of Thy compassions, blot out my transgression. Wash me still more from mine iniquity, and cleanse me from my sin. For I acknowledge my iniquity, and my sin is ever before me. Against Thee only have I sinned, and done that which was evil in Thy sight; that Thou mayest be justified in Thy sayings, and mayest overcome when Thou[3] art judged. For, behold, I was conceived in transgressions, and in my sins did my mother conceive me. For, behold, Thou hast loved truth; the secret and hidden things of wisdom hast Thou shown me. Thou shalt sprinkle me with hyssop, and I shall be cleansed; Thou shalt wash me, and I shall be whiter than snow. Thou shalt make me to hear joy and gladness; my bones, which have been humbled, shall exult. Turn away Thy face from my sins, and blot out all mine iniquities. Create in me a clean heart, O God, and renew a right spirit within me.[4] Cast me not away from Thy presence, and take not Thy Holy Spirit from me. Restore to me the joy of Thy salvation, and establish me by Thy governing Spirit. I will teach transgressors Thy ways, and the ungodly shall be

---

1. Or, as some render, "to whom."
2. Ps. 89:21
3. Or, "when Thou judgest."
4. Literally, "in my inwards."

converted unto Thee. Deliver me from blood-guiltiness,[5] O God, the God of my salvation: my tongue shall exult in Thy righteousness. O Lord, Thou shalt open my mouth, and my lips shall show forth Thy praise. For if Thou hadst desired sacrifice, I would have given it; Thou wilt not delight in burnt-offerings. The sacrifice [acceptable] to God is a bruised spirit; a broken and a contrite heart God will not despise.[6]

---

5. Literally, "bloods."
6. Ps. 51:1–17.

CHAPTER XIX

Imitating These Examples, Let Us Seek After Peace

THUS THE HUMILITY and godly submission of so great and illustrious men have rendered not only us, but also all the generations before us, better; even as many as have received His oracles in fear and truth. Wherefore, having so many great and glorious examples set before us, let us turn again to the practice of that peace which from the beginning was the mark set before us;[1] and let us look steadfastly to the Father and Creator of the universe, and cleave to His mighty and surpassingly great gifts and benefactions, of peace. Let us contemplate Him with our understanding, and look with the eyes of our soul to His long-suffering will. Let us reflect how free from wrath He is towards all His creation.

---

1. Literally, "Becoming partakers of many great and glorious deeds, let us return to the aim of peace delivered to us from the beginning." Comp. Heb. 12:1

CHAPTER XX

The Peace And Harmony Of The Universe

THE HEAVENS, REVOLVING under His government, are subject to Him in peace. Day and night run the course appointed by Him, in no wise hindering each other. The sun and moon, with the companies of the stars, roll on in harmony according to His command, within their prescribed limits, and without any deviation. The fruitful earth, according to His will, brings forth food in abundance, at the proper seasons, for man and beast and all the living beings upon it, never hesitating, nor changing any of the ordinances which He has fixed. The unsearchable places of abysses, and the indescribable arrangements of the lower world, are restrained by the same laws. The vast unmeasurable sea, gathered together by His working into various basins,[1] never passes beyond the bounds placed around it, but does as He has commanded. For He said, "Thus far shalt thou come, and thy waves shall be broken within thee."[2] The ocean, impassible to man, and the worlds beyond it, are regulated by the same enactments of the Lord. The seasons of spring, summer, autumn, and winter, peacefully give place to one another. The winds in their several quarters[3] fulfil, at the proper time, their service without hindrance. The ever-flowing fountains, formed both for enjoyment and health, furnish without fail their breasts for the life of men. The very smallest of living beings meet together in peace and concord. All these the great Creator and Lord of all has appointed to exist in peace and harmony; while He does good to all, but most abundantly to us who have fled for ref-

1. Or, "collections."
2. Job 38:11
3. Or, "stations."

uge to His compassions through Jesus Christ our Lord, to whom be glory and majesty for ever and ever. Amen.

CHAPTER XXI

Let Us Obey God, And Not The Authors Of Sedition

TAKE HEED, BELOVED, lest His many kindnesses lead to the condemnation of us all. [For thus it must be] unless we walk worthy of Him, and with one mind do those things which are good and well-pleasing in His sight. For [the Scripture] saith in a certain place, "The Spirit of the Lord is a candle searching the secret parts of the belly."[1] Let us reflect how near He is, and that none of the thoughts or reasonings in which we engage are hid from Him. It is right, therefore, that we should not leave the post which His will has assigned us. Let us rather offend those men who are foolish, and inconsiderate, and lifted up, and who glory in the pride of their speech, than [offend] God. Let us reverence the Lord Jesus Christ, whose blood was given for us; let us esteem those who have the rule over us;[2] let us honour the aged[3] among us; let us train up the young men in the fear of God; let us direct our wives to that which is good. Let them exhibit the lovely habit of purity [in all their conduct]; let them show forth the sincere disposition of meekness; let them make manifest the command which they have of their tongue, by their manner[4] of speaking; let them display their love, not by preferring[5] one to another, but by showing equal affection to all that piously fear God. Let your children be partakers of true Christian training; let them learn of how great avail humility is with God – how much the spirit of pure affection

---

1. Prov. 20:27
2. Comp. Heb. 13:17; 1 Thess. 5:12-13.
3. Or, "the presbyters."
4. Some read, "by their silence."
5. Comp. 1 Tim. 5:21

can prevail with Him – how excellent and great His fear is, and how it saves all those who walk in⁶ it with a pure mind. For He is a Searcher of the thoughts and desires [of the heart]: His breath is in us; and when He pleases, He will take it away.

---

6. Some translate, "who turn to Him."

CHAPTER XXII

These Exhortations Are Confirmed By The Christian Faith, Which Proclaims The Misery Of Sinful Conduct

Now THE FAITH which is in Christ confirms all these [admonitions]. For He Himself by the Holy Ghost thus addresses us:

> Come, you children, hearken unto Me; I will teach you the fear of the Lord. What man is he that desireth life, and loveth to see good days? Keep thy tongue from evil, and thy lips from speaking guile. Depart from evil, and do good; seek peace, and pursue it. The eyes of the Lord are upon the righteous, and His ears are [open] unto their prayers. The face of the Lord is against them that do evil, to cut off the remembrance of them from the earth. The righteous cried, and the Lord heard him, and delivered him out of all his troubles.[1]

"Many are the stripes [appointed for] the wicked; but mercy shall compass those about who hope in the Lord."[2]

---

1. Ps. 34:11–17
2. Ps. 32:10

CHAPTER XXIII

Be Humble, And Believe That Christ Will Come Again

THE ALL-MERCIFUL and beneficent Father has bowels [of compassion] towards those that fear Him, and kindly and lovingly bestows His favours upon those who come to Him with a simple mind. Wherefore let us not be double-minded; neither let our soul be lifted[1] up on account of His exceedingly great and glorious gifts. Far from us be that which is written,

> Wretched are they who are of a double mind, and of a doubting heart; who say, These things we have heard even in the times of our fathers; but, behold, we have grown old, and none of them has happened unto us.[2]

You foolish ones! compare yourselves to a tree: take [for instance] the vine. First of all, it sheds its leaves, then it buds, next it puts forth leaves, and then it flowers; after that comes the sour grape, and then follows the ripened fruit. You perceive how in a little time the fruit of a tree comes to maturity. Of a truth, soon and suddenly shall His will be accomplished, as the Scripture also bears witness, saying, "Speedily will He come, and will not tarry;"[3] and, "The Lord shall suddenly come to His temple, even the Holy One, for whom you look."[4]

---

1. Or, as some render, "neither let us have any doubt of."
2. Some regard these words as taken from an apocryphal book, others as derived from a fusion of Jas. 1:8 and 2 Pet. 3:3-4.
3. Hab. 2:3; Heb. 10:37
4. Mal. 3:1

CHAPTER XXIV

God Continually Shows Us In Nature That There Will Be A Resurrection

LET US CONSIDER, beloved, how the Lord continually proves to us that there shall be a future resurrection, of which He has rendered the Lord Jesus Christ the first-fruits[1] by raising Him from the dead. Let us contemplate, beloved, the resurrection which is at all times taking place. Day and night declare to us a resurrection. The night sinks to sleep, and the day arises; the day [again] departs, and the night comes on. Let us behold the fruits [of the earth], how the sowing of grain takes place. The sower[2] goes forth, and casts it into the ground; and the seed being thus scattered, though dry and naked when it fell upon the earth, is gradually dissolved. Then out of its dissolution the mighty power of the providence of the Lord raises it up again, and from one seed many arise and bring forth fruit.

---

1. Comp. 1 Cor. 15:20; Col. 1:18.
2. Comp. Luke 8:5.

CHAPTER XXV

The Phoenix An Emblem Of Our Resurrection

LET US CONSIDER that wonderful sign [of the resurrection] which takes place in Eastern lands, that is, in Arabia and the countries round about. There is a certain bird which is called a phoenix. This is the only one of its kind, and lives five hundred years. And when the time of its dissolution draws near that it must die, it builds itself a nest of frankincense, and myrrh, and other spices, into which, when the time is fulfilled, it enters and dies. But as the flesh decays a certain kind of worm is produced, which, being nourished by the juices of the dead bird, brings forth feathers. Then, when it has acquired strength, it takes up that nest in which are the bones of its parent, and bearing these it passes from the land of Arabia into Egypt, to the city called Heliopolis. And, in open day, flying in the sight of all men, it places them on the altar of the sun, and having done this, hastens back to its former abode. The priests then inspect the registers of the dates, and find that it has returned exactly as the five hundredth year was completed.[1]

---

1. This fable respecting the phoenix is mentioned by Herodotus (ii. 73) and by Pliny (*Nat. Hist.*, x. 2) and is used as above by Tertullian (*De Resurr.*, §13) and by others of the Fathers.

CHAPTER XXVI

We Shall Rise Again, Then, As The Scripture Also Testifies

Do WE THEN DEEM it any great and wonderful thing for the Maker of all things to raise up again those that have piously served Him in the assurance of a good faith, when even by a bird He shows us the mightiness of His power to fulfil His promise?[1] For [the Scripture] saith in a certain place, "Thou shalt raise me up, and I shall confess unto Thee;"[2] and again, "I laid me down, and slept; I awaked, because Thou art with me;"[3] and again, Job says, "Thou shalt raise up this flesh of mine, which has suffered all these things."[4]

---

1. Literally, "the mightiness of His promise."
2. Ps. 28:7, or some apocryphal book.
3. Comp. Ps. 3:6.
4. Job 29:25-26

CHAPTER XXVII

In The Hope Of The Resurrection, Let Us Cleave To The Omnipotent And Omniscient God

HAVING THEN THIS HOPE, let our souls be bound to Him who is faithful in His promises, and just in His judgments. He who has commanded us not to lie, shall much more Himself not lie; for nothing is impossible with God, except to lie.[1] Let His faith therefore be stirred up again within us, and let us consider that all things are nigh unto Him. By the word of His might[2] He established all things, and by His word He can overthrow them. "Who shall say unto Him, What hast thou done? or, Who shall resist the power of His strength?"[3] When and as He pleases He will do all things, and none of the things determined by Him shall pass away.[4] All things are open before Him, and nothing can be hidden from His counsel. "The heavens[5] declare the glory of God, and the firmament showeth His handiwork. Day unto day uttereth speech, and night unto night showeth knowledge. And there are no words or speeches of which the voices are not heard."[6]

---

1. Comp. Tit. 1:2; Heb. 6:18.
2. Or, "majesty."
3. Wisdom 12:12, Wisdom 11:22.
4. Comp. Matt. 24:35.
5. Literally, "If the heavens," etc.
6. Ps. 19:1-3.

CHAPTER XXVIII

God Sees All Things: Therefore Let Us Avoid Transgression

SINCE THEN ALL THINGS are seen and heard [by God], let us fear Him, and forsake those wicked works which proceed from evil desires;[1] so that, through His mercy, we may be protected from the judgments to come. For whither can any of us flee from His mighty hand? Or what world will receive any of those who run away from Him? For the Scripture saith in a certain place,

> Whither shall I go, and where shall I be hid from Thy presence? If I ascend into heaven, Thou art there; if I go away even to the uttermost parts of the earth, there is Thy right hand; if I make my bed in the abyss, there is Thy Spirit.[2]

Whither, then, shall any one go, or where shall he escape from Him who comprehends all things?

---

1. Literally, "abominable lusts of evil deeds."
2. Ps. 139:7-10

CHAPTER XXIX

Let Us Also Draw Near To God In Purity Of Heart

LET US THEN DRAW near to Him with holiness of spirit, lifting up pure and undefiled hands unto Him, loving our gracious and merciful Father, who has made us partakers in the blessings of His elect.[1] For thus it is written,

> When the Most High divided the nations, when He scattered[2] the sons of Adam, He fixed the bounds of the nations according to the number of the angels of God. His people Jacob became the portion of the Lord, and Israel the lot of His inheritance.[3]

And in another place [the Scripture] saith, "Behold, the Lord taketh unto Himself a nation out of the midst of the nations, as a man takes the first-fruits of his threshing-floor; and from that nation shall come forth the Most Holy."[4]

---

1. Literally "has made us to Himself a part of election."
2. Literally, "sowed abroad."
3. Deut. 32:8-9
4. Formed apparently from Num. 18:27 and 2 Chron. 31:14. Literally, the closing words are, "the holy of holies."

CHAPTER XXX

Let Us Do Those Things That Please God, And Flee From Those He Hates, That We May Be Blessed

SEEING, THEREFORE, that we are the portion of the Holy One, let us do all those things which pertain to holiness, avoiding all evil-speaking, all abominable and impure embraces, together with all drunkenness, seeking after change,[1] all abominable lusts, detestable adultery, and execrable pride. "For God," saith [the Scripture], "resisteth the proud, but giveth grace to the humble."[2] Let us cleave, then, to those to whom grace has been given by God. Let us clothe ourselves with concord and humility, ever exercising self-control, standing far off from all whispering and evil-speaking, being justified by our works, and not our words. For [the Scripture] saith, "He that speaketh much, shall also hear much in answer. And does he that is ready in speech deem himself righteous? Blessed is he that is born of woman, who liveth but a short time: be not given to much speaking."[3] Let our praise be in God, and not of ourselves; for God hateth those that commend themselves. Let testimony to our good deeds be borne by others, as it was in the case of our righteous forefathers. Boldness, and arrogance, and audacity belong to those that are accursed of God; but moderation, humility, and meekness to such as are blessed by Him.

---

1. Some translate, "youthful lusts."
2. Prov. 3:34; Jas. 4:6; 1 Pet. 5:5.
3. Job 11:2-3. The translation is doubtful. [But see Septuagint.]

CHAPTER XXXI

Let Us See By What Means We May Obtain The Divine Blessing

LET US CLEAVE THEN to His blessing, and consider what are the means[1] of possessing it. Let us think[2] over the things which have taken place from the beginning. For what reason was our father Abraham blessed? Was it not because he wrought righteousness and truth through faith?[3] Isaac, with perfect confidence, as if knowing what was to happen,[4] cheerfully yielded himself as a sacrifice[5] Jacob, through reason[6] of his brother, went forth with humility from his own land, and came to Laban and served him; and there was given to him the sceptre of the twelve tribes of Israel.

---

1. Literally, "what are the ways of His blessing."
2. Literally, "unroll."
3. Comp. Jas. 2:21.
4. Some translate, "knowing what was to come."
5. Gen. 22
6. So Jacobson: Wotton reads, "fleeing from his brother."

CHAPTER XXXII

We Are Justified Not By Our Own Works, But By Faith

Whosoever will candidly consider each particular, will recognize the greatness of the gifts which were given by him.[1] For from him[2] have sprung the priests and all the Levites who minister at the altar of God. From him also [was descended] our Lord Jesus Christ according to the flesh.[3] From him [arose] kings, princes, and rulers of the race of Judah. Nor are his other tribes in small glory, inasmuch as God had promised, "Thy seed shall be as the stars of heaven."[4] All these, therefore, were highly honoured, and made great, not for their own sake, or for their own works, or for the righteousness which they wrought, but through the operation of His will. And we, too, being called by His will in Christ Jesus, are not justified by ourselves, nor by our own wisdom, or understanding, or godliness, or works which we have wrought in holiness of heart; but by that faith through which, from the beginning, Almighty God has justified all men; to whom be glory for ever and ever. Amen.

---

1. The meaning is here very doubtful. Some translate, "the gifts which were given to Jacob by Him," i.e., God.
2. MS. αὐτῶν, referring to the gifts: we have followed the emendation αὐτοῦ, adopted by most editors. Some refer the word to *God*, and not *Jacob*.
3. Comp. Rom. 9:5.
4. Gen. 22:17, Gen. 28:4.

CHAPTER XXXIII

But Let Us Not Owe Up The Practice Of Good Works And Love: God Himself Is An Example To Us Of Good Works

WHAT SHALL WE DO, then, brethren? Shall we become slothful in well-doing, and cease from the practice of love? God forbid that any such course should be followed by us! But rather let us hasten with all energy and readiness of mind to perform every good work. For the Creator and Lord of all Himself rejoices in His works. For by His infinitely great power He established the heavens, and by His incomprehensible wisdom He adorned them. He also divided the earth from the water which surrounds it, and fixed it upon the immoveable foundation of His own will. The animals also which are upon it He commanded by His own word[1] into existence. So likewise, when He had formed the sea, and the living creatures which are in it, He enclosed them [within their proper bounds] by His own power. Above all,[2] with His holy and undefiled hands He formed man, the most excellent [of His creatures], and truly great through the understanding given him – the express likeness of His own image. For thus says God: "Let us make man in Our image, and after Our likeness. So God made man; male and female He created them."[3] Having thus finished all these things, He approved them, and blessed them, and said, "Increase and multiply."[4] We

---

1. Or, "commandment."
2. Or, "in addition to all."
3. Gen. 1:26-27
4. Gen. 1:28.

see,[5] then, how all righteous men have been adorned with good works, and how the Lord Himself, adorning Himself with His works, rejoiced. Having therefore such an example, let us without delay accede to His will, and let us work the work of righteousness with our whole strength.

---

5. Or, "let us consider."

CHAPTER XXXIV

Great Is The Reward Of Good Works With God: Joined Together In Harmony, Let Us Implore That Reward From Him

THE GOOD SERVANT[1] receives the bread of his labour with confidence; the lazy and slothful cannot look his employer in the face. It is requisite, therefore, that we be prompt in the practice of well-doing; for of Him are all things. And thus He forewarns us: "Behold, the Lord [cometh], and His reward is before His face, to render to every man according to his work."[2] He exhorts us, therefore, with our whole heart to attend to this,[3] that we be not lazy or slothful in any good work. Let our boasting and our confidence be in Him. Let us submit ourselves to His will. Let us consider the whole multitude of His angels, how they stand ever ready to minister to His will. For the Scripture saith, "Ten thousand times ten thousand stood around Him, and thousands of thousands ministered unto Him,[4] and cried, Holy, holy, holy, [is] the Lord of Sabaoth; the whole creation is full of His glory."[5] And let us therefore, conscientiously gathering together in harmony, cry to Him earnestly, as with one mouth, that we may be made partakers of His great and glorious promises. For [the Scripture] saith, "Eyes hath not seen, nor ear heard, neither have entered into

---

1. Or, "labourer."
2. Isa. 40:10, Isa. 62:11; Rev. 22:12
3. The text here seems to be corrupt. Some translate, "He warns us with all His heart to this end, that," etc.
4. Dan. 7:10
5. Isa. 6:3

the heart of man, the things which He hath prepared for them that wait for Him."[6]

---

6. 1 Cor. 2:9

CHAPTER XXXV

Immense Is This Reward: How Shall We Obtain It?

How BLESSED and wonderful, beloved, are the gifts of God! Life in immortality, splendour in righteousness, truth in perfect confidence,[1] faith in assurance, self-control in holiness! And all these fall under the cognizance of our understandings [now]; what then shall those things be which are prepared for such as wait for Him? The Creator and Father of all worlds,[2] the Most Holy, alone knows their amount and their beauty. Let us therefore earnestly strive to be found in the number of those that wait for Him, in order that we may share in His promised gifts. But how, beloved, shall this be done? If our understanding be fixed by faith rewards God; if we earnestly seek the things which are pleasing and acceptable to Him; if we do the things which are in harmony with His blameless will; and if we follow the way of truth, casting away from us all unrighteousness and iniquity, along with all covetousness, strife, evil practices, deceit, whispering, and evil-speaking, all hatred of God, pride and haughtiness, vainglory and ambition.[3] For they that do such things are hateful to God; and not only they that do them, but also those that take pleasure in them that do them.[4] For the Scripture saith,

But to the sinner God said, Wherefore dost thou declare my statutes, and take my covenant into thy mouth, seeing thou hatest instruction, and castest my words behind thee? When thou sawest

---

1. Some translate, "in liberty."
2. Or, "of the ages."
3. The reading is doubtful: some have ἀφιλοξενίαν, "want of a hospitable spirit." [So Jacobson.]
4. Rom. 1:32

a thief, thou consentedst with[5] him, and didst make thy portion with adulterers. Thy mouth has abounded with wickedness, and thy tongue contrived[6] deceit. Thou sittest, and speakest against thy brother; thou slanderest[7] thine own mother›s son. These things thou hast done, and I kept silence; thou thoughtest, wicked one, that I should be like to thyself. But I will reprove thee, and set thyself before thee. Consider now these things, you that forget God, lest He tear you in pieces, like a lion, and there be none to deliver. The sacrifice of praise will glorify Me, and a way is there by which I will show him the salvation of God.[8]

---

5. Literally, "didst run with."
6. Literally, "didst weave."
7. Or, "layest a snare for."
8. Ps. l. 16–23. The reader will observe how the Septuagint followed by Clement differs from the Hebrew.

CHAPTER XXXVI

All Blessings Are Given To Us Through Christ

THIS IS THE WAY, beloved, in which we find our Saviour,[1] even Jesus Christ, the High Priest of all our offerings, the defender and helper of our infirmity. By Him we look up to the heights of heaven. By Him we behold, as in a glass, His immaculate and most excellent visage. By Him are the eyes of our hearts opened. By Him our foolish and darkened understanding blossoms[2] up anew towards His marvellous light. By Him the Lord has willed that we should taste of immortal knowledge,[3] "who, being the brightness of His majesty, is by so much greater than the angels, as He hath by inheritance obtained a more excellent name than they."[4] For it is thus written, "Who maketh His angels spirits, and His ministers a flame of fire."[5] But concerning His Son[6] the Lord spoke thus: "Thou art my Son, to-day have I begotten Thee. Ask of Me, and I will give Thee the heathen for Thine inheritance, and the uttermost parts of the earth for Thy possession."[7] And again He saith to Him, "Sit Thou at My right hand, until I make Thine enemies Thy footstool."[8] But who are His enemies? All the wicked, and those who set themselves to oppose the will of God.[9]

---

1. Literally, "that which saves us."
2. Or, "rejoices to behold."
3. Or, "knowledge of immortality."
4. Heb. 1:3-4
5. Ps. 104:4; Heb. 1:7.
6. Some render, "to the Son."
7. Ps. 2:7-8; Heb. 1:5
8. Ps. 110:1; Heb. 1:13.
9. Some read, "who oppose their own will to that of God."

CHAPTER XXXVII

Christ Is Our Leader, And We His Soldiers

LET US THEN, men and brethren, with all energy act the part of soldiers, in accordance with His holy commandments. Let us consider those who serve under our generals, with what order, obedience, and submissiveness they perform the things which are commanded them. All are not prefects, nor commanders of a thousand, nor of a hundred, nor of fifty, nor the like, but each one in his own rank performs the things commanded by the king and the generals. The great cannot subsist without the small, nor the small without the great. There is a kind of mixture in all things, and thence arises mutual advantage.[1] Let us take our body for an example.[2] The head is nothing without the feet, and the feet are nothing without the head; yea, the very smallest members of our body are necessary and useful to the whole body. But all work[3] harmoniously together, and are under one common rule[4] for the preservation of the whole body.

---

1. Literally, "in these there is use."
2. 1 Cor. 12:12, etc.
3. Literally, "all breathe together."
4. Literally, "use one subjection."

CHAPTER XXXVIII

Let The Members Of The Church Submit Themselves, And No One Exalt Himself Above Another

LET OUR WHOLE BODY, then, be preserved in, Christ Jesus; and let every one be subject to his neighbour, according to the special gift[1] bestowed upon him. Let the strong not despise the weak, and let the weak show respect unto the strong. Let the rich man provide for the wants of the poor; and let the poor man bless God, because He hath given him one by whom his need may be supplied. Let the wise man display his wisdom, not by [mere] words, but through good deeds. Let the humble not bear testimony to himself, but leave witness to be borne to him by another.[2] Let him that is pure in the flesh not grow proud[3] of it, and boast, knowing that it was another who bestowed on him the gift of continence. Let us consider, then, brethren, of what matter we were made, – who and what manner of beings we came into the world, as it were out of a sepulchre, and from utter darkness.[4] He who made us and fashioned us, having prepared His bountiful gifts for us before we were born, introduced us into His world. Since, therefore, we receive all these things from Him, we ought for everything to give Him thanks; to whom be glory for ever and ever. Amen.

---

1. Literally, "according as he has been placed in his charism."
2. Comp. Prov. 27:2.
3. The ms. is here slightly torn, and we are left to conjecture.
4. Comp. Ps. 139:15.

CHAPTER XXXIX

There Is No Reason For Self-Conceit

FOOLISH AND INCONSIDERATE MEN, who have neither wisdom[1] nor instruction, mock and deride us, being eager to exalt themselves in their own conceits. For what can a mortal man do? Or what strength is there in one made out of the dust? For it is written,

> There was no shape before mine eyes, only I heard a sound,[2] and a voice [saying], What then? Shall a man be pure before the Lord? or shall such an one be [counted] blameless in his deeds, seeing He does not confide in His servants, and has charged[3] even His angels with perversity? The heaven is not clean in His sight: how much less they that dwell in houses of clay, of which also we ourselves were made! He smote them as a moth; and from morning even until evening they endure not. Because they could furnish no assistance to themselves, they perished. He breathed upon them, and they died, because they had no wisdom. But call now, if any one will answer thee, or if thou wilt look to any of the holy angels; for wrath destroys the foolish man, and envy killeth him that is in error. I have seen the foolish taking root, but their habitation was presently consumed. Let their sons be far from safety; let them be despised[4] before the gates of those less than themselves, and there shall be none to deliver. For what was prepared for them, the righteous shall eat; and they shall not be delivered from evil.[5]

---

1. Literally, "and silly and uninstructed."
2. Literally, "a breath."
3. Or, "has perceived."
4. Some render, "they perished at the gates."
5. Job 4:16-18, Job 15:15, Job 4:19-21, Job 5:1-5.

CHAPTER XL

Let Us Preserve In The Church The Order Appointed By God

THESE THINGS THEREFORE being manifest to us, and since we look into the depths of the divine knowledge, it behooves us to do all things in [their proper] order, which the Lord has commanded us to perform at stated times.[1] He has enjoined offerings [to be presented] and service to be performed [to Him], and that not thoughtlessly or irregularly, but at the appointed times and hours. Where and by whom He desires these things to be done, He Himself has fixed by His own supreme will, in order that all things being piously done according to His good pleasure, may be acceptable unto Him.[2] Those, therefore, who present their offerings at the appointed times, are accepted and blessed; for inasmuch as they follow the laws of the Lord, they sin not. For his own peculiar services are assigned to the high priest, and their own proper place is prescribed to the priests, and their own special ministrations devolve on the Levites. The layman is bound by the laws that pertain to laymen.

---

1. Some join κατὰ καιροὺς τεταγμένους, "at stated times." to the next sentence. [1 Cor. 16:1-2]
2. Literally, "to His will." [Comp. Rom. 15:15-16, Greek]

CHAPTER XLI

Continuation Of The Same Subject

LET EVERY ONE OF YOU, brethren, give thanks to God in his own order, living in all good conscience, with becoming gravity, and not going beyond the rule of the ministry prescribed to him. Not in every place, brethren, are the daily sacrifices offered, or the peace-offerings, or the sin-offerings and the trespass-offerings, but in Jerusalem only. And even there they are not offered in any place, but only at the altar before the temple, that which is offered being first carefully examined by the high priest and the ministers already mentioned. Those, therefore, who do anything beyond that which is agreeable to His will, are punished with death. You see,[1] brethren, that the greater the knowledge that has been vouchsafed to us, the greater also is the danger to which we are exposed.

---

1. Or, "consider." [This chapter has been cited to prove the earlier date for this Epistle. But the reference to Jerusalem may be an ideal present.]

CHAPTER XLII

The Order Of Ministers In The Church

THE APOSTLES HAVE preached the Gospel to us from[1] the Lord Jesus Christ; Jesus Christ [has done so] from[2] God. Christ therefore was sent forth by God, and the apostles by Christ. Both these appointments,[3] then, were made in an orderly way, according to the will of God. Having therefore received their orders, and being fully assured by the resurrection of our Lord Jesus Christ, and established[4] in the word of God, with full assurance of the Holy Ghost, they went forth proclaiming that the kingdom of God was at hand. And thus preaching through countries and cities, they appointed the first-fruits [of their labours], having first proved them by the Spirit,[5] to be bishops and deacons of those who should afterwards believe. Nor was this any new thing, since indeed many ages before it was written concerning bishops and deacons. For thus saith the Scripture in a certain place, "I will appoint their bishops[6] in righteousness, and their deacons[7] in faith."[8]

---

1. Or, "by the command of."
2. Or, "by the command of."
3. Literally, "both things were done."
4. Or, "confirmed by."
5. Or, "having tested them in spirit."
6. Or, "overseers."
7. Or, "servants."
8. Isa. 60:17, Septuagint; but the text is here altered by Clement. The LXX. have "I will give thy rulers in peace, and thy overseers in righteousness."

CHAPTER XLIII

Moses Of Old Stilled The Contention Which Arose Concerning The Priestly Dignity

AND WHAT WONDER is it if those in Christ who were entrusted with such a duty by God, appointed those [ministers] before mentioned, when the blessed Moses also, "a faithful servant in all his house,"[1] noted down in the sacred books all the injunctions which were given him, and when the other prophets also followed him, bearing witness with one consent to the ordinances which he had appointed? For, when rivalry arose concerning the priesthood, and the tribes were contending among themselves as to which of them should be adorned with that glorious title, he commanded the twelve princes of the tribes to bring him their rods, each one being inscribed with the name[2] of the tribe. And he took them and bound them [together], and sealed them with the rings of the princes of the tribes, and laid them up in the tabernacle of witness on the table of God. And having shut the doors of the tabernacle, he sealed the keys, as he had done the rods, and said to them, Men and brethren, the tribe whose rod shall blossom has God chosen to fulfil the office of the priesthood, and to minister unto Him. And when the morning was come, he assembled all Israel, six hundred thousand men, and showed the seals to the princes of the tribes, and opened the tabernacle of witness, and brought forth the rods. And the rod of Aaron was found not only to have blossomed, but to bear fruit upon it.[3] What think you, beloved? Did not Moses

---

1. Num. xii. 7; Heb. iii. 5.
2. Literally, "every tribe being written according to its name."
3. See Num. xvii.

know beforehand that this would happen? Undoubtedly he knew; but he acted thus, that there might be no sedition in Israel, and that the name of the true and only God might be glorified; to whom be glory for ever and ever. Amen.

CHAPTER XLIV

The Ordinances Of The Apostles, That There Might Be No Contention Respecting The Priestly Office

OUR APOSTLES ALSO KNEW, through our Lord Jesus Christ, and there would be strife on account of the office[1] of the episcopate. For this reason, therefore, inasmuch as they had obtained a perfect fore-knowledge of this, they appointed those [ministers] already mentioned, and afterwards gave instructions,[2] that when these should fall asleep, other approved men should succeed them in their ministry. We are of opinion, therefore, that those appointed by them,[3] or afterwards by other eminent men, with the consent of the whole Church, and who have blamelessly served the flock of Christ in a humble, peaceable, and disinterested spirit, and have for a long time possessed the good opinion of all, cannot be justly dismissed from the ministry. For our sin will not be small, if we eject from the episcopate[4] those who have blamelessly and

1. Literally, "on account of the title of the oversight." Some understand this to mean, "in regard to the dignity of the episcopate;" and others simply, "on account of the oversight."
2. The meaning of this passage is much controverted. Some render, "left a list of other approved persons;" while others translate the unusual word ἐπινομή, which causes the difficulty, by "testamentary direction," and many others deem the text corrupt. We have given what seems the simplest version of the text as it stands. [Comp. the versions of Wake, Chevallier, and others.]
3. i.e., the apostles.
4. Or, "oversight."

holily fulfilled its duties.[5] Blessed are those presbyters who, having finished their course before now, have obtained a fruitful and perfect departure [from this world]; for they have no fear lest any one deprive them of the place now appointed them. But we see that you have removed some men of excellent behaviour from the ministry, which they fulfilled blamelessly and with honour.

---

5. Literally, "presented the offerings."

CHAPTER XLV

It Is The Part Of The Wicked To Vex The Righteous

YOU ARE FOND OF CONTENTION, brethren, and full of zeal about things which do not pertain to salvation. Look carefully into the Scriptures, which are the true utterances of the Holy Spirit. Observe[1] that nothing of an unjust or counterfeit character is written in them. There[2] you will not find that the righteous were cast off by men who themselves were holy. The righteous were indeed persecuted, but only by the wicked. They were cast into prison, but only by the unholy; they were stoned, but only by transgressors; they were slain, but only by the accursed, and such as had conceived an unrighteous envy against them. Exposed to such sufferings, they endured them gloriously. For what shall we say, brethren? Was Daniel[3] cast into the den of lions by such as feared God? Were Ananias, and Azarias, and Mishael shut up in a furnace[4] of fire by those who observed[5] the great and glorious worship of the Most High? Far from us be such a thought! Who, then, were they that did such things? The hateful, and those full of all wickedness, were roused to such a pitch of fury, that they inflicted torture on those who served God with a holy and blameless purpose [of heart], not knowing that the Most High is the Defender and Protector of all such as with a pure conscience venerate[6] His all-excellent name; to whom be glory for ever and ever. Amen. But

---

1. Or, "Ye perceive."
2. Or, "For."
3. Dan. 6:16
4. Dan. 3:20
5. Literally, "worshipped."
6. Literally, "serve."

they who with confidence endured [these things] are now heirs of glory and honour, and have been exalted and made illustrious[7] by God in their memorial for ever and ever. Amen.

---

7. Or, "lifted up."

CHAPTER XLVI

Let Us Cleave To The Righteous: Your Strife Is Pernicious

SUCH EXAMPLES, therefore, brethren, it is right that we should follow;[1] since it is written, "Cleave to the holy, for those that cleave to them shall [themselves] be made holy."[2] And again, in another place, [the Scripture] saith, "With a harmless man thou shalt prove[3] thyself harmless, and with an elect man thou shalt be elect, and with a perverse man thou shalt show[4] thyself perverse."[5] Let us cleave, therefore, to the innocent and righteous, since these are the elect of God. Why are there strifes, and tumults, and divisions, and schisms, and wars[6] among you? Have we not [all] one God and one Christ? Is there not one Spirit of grace poured out upon us? And have we not one calling in Christ?[7] Why do we divide and tear to pieces the members of Christ, and raise up strife against our own body, and have reached such a height of madness as to forget that "we are members one of another?"[8] Remember the words of our Lord Jesus Christ, how[9] He said,

---

1. Literally, "To such examples it is right that we should cleave."
2. Not found in Scripture.
3. Literally, "be."
4. Or, "thou wilt overthrow."
5. Ps. 18:25, 26.
6. Or, "war." Comp. Jas. 4:1.
7. Comp. Eph. 4:4-6.
8. Rom. 12:5.
9. This clause is wanting in the text.

Woe to that man [by whom[10] offences come]! It were better for him that he had never been born, than that he should cast a stumbling-block before one of my elect. Yea, it were better for him that a millstone should be hung about [his neck], and he should be sunk in the depths of the sea, than that he should cast a stumbling-block before one of my little ones."[11]

Your schism has subverted [the faith of] many, has discouraged many, has given rise to doubt in many, and has caused grief to us all. And still your sedition continueth.

---

10. This clause is wanting in the text.
11. Comp. Matt. 18:6, Matt. 26:24; Mark 9:42; Luke 17:2.

CHAPTER XLVII

Your Recent Discord Is Worse Than The Former Which Took Place In The Times Of Paul

TAKE UP THE EPISTLE of the blessed Apostle Paul. What did he write to you at the time when the Gospel first began to be preached?[1] Truly, under the inspiration[2] of the Spirit, he wrote to you concerning himself, and Cephas, and Apollos,[3] because even then parties[4] had been formed among you. But that inclination for one above another entailed less guilt upon you, inasmuch as your partialities were then shown towards apostles, already of high reputation, and towards a man whom they had approved. But now reflect who those are that have perverted you, and lessened the renown of your far-famed brotherly love. It is disgraceful, beloved, yea, highly disgraceful, and unworthy of your Christian profession,[5] that such a thing should be heard of as that the most steadfast and ancient Church of the Corinthians should, on account of one or two persons, engage in sedition against its presbyters. And this rumour has reached not only us, but those also who are unconnected[6] with us; so that, through your infatuation, the name of the Lord is blasphemed, while danger is also brought upon yourselves.

---

1. Literally, "in the beginning of the Gospel." [Comp. Phil. 4:15]
2. Or, "spiritually."
3. 1 Cor. 3:13, etc.
4. Or, "inclinations for one above another."
5. Literally, "of conduct in Christ."
6. Or, "aliens from us," i.e., the Gentiles.

CHAPTER XLVIII

Let Us Return To The Practice Of Brotherly Love

LET US THEREFORE, with all haste, put an end[1] to this [state of things]; and let us fall down before the Lord, and beseech Him with tears, that He would mercifully[2] be reconciled to us, and restore us to our former seemly and holy practice of brotherly love. For [such conduct] is the gate of righteousness, which is set open for the attainment of life, as it is written, "Open to me the gates of righteousness; I will go in by them, and will praise the Lord: this is the gate of the Lord: the righteous shall enter in by it."[3] Although, therefore, many gates have been set open, yet this gate of righteousness is that gate in Christ by which blessed are all they that have entered in and have directed their way in holiness and righteousness, doing all things without disorder. Let a man be faithful: let him be powerful in the utterance of knowledge; let him be wise in judging of words; let him be pure in all his deeds; yet the more he seems to be superior to others [in these respects], the more humble-minded ought he to be, and to seek the common good of all, and not merely his own advantage.

---

1. Literally "remove."
2. Literally, "becoming merciful."
3. Ps. 118:19-20.

CHAPTER XLIX

The Praise Of Love

LET HIM WHO HAS LOVE in Christ keep the commandments of Christ. Who can describe the [blessed] bond of the love of God? What man is able to tell the excellence of its beauty, as it ought to be told? The height to which love exalts is unspeakable. Love unites us to God. Love covers a multitude of sins.[1] Love beareth all things, is long-suffering in all things.[2] There is nothing base, nothing arrogant in love. Love admits of no schisms: love gives rise to no seditions: love does all things in harmony. By love have all the elect of God been made perfect; without love nothing is well-pleasing to God. In love has the Lord taken us to Himself. On account of the Love he bore us, Jesus Christ our Lord gave His blood for us by the will of God; His flesh for our flesh, and His soul for our souls.[3]

---

1. Jas. 5:20; 1 Pet. 4:8.
2. Comp. 1 Cor. 13:4, etc.
3. [Comp. Irenæus, v. 1; also Mathetes, Ep. to Diognetus, cap. ix.]

CHAPTER L

Let Us Pray To Be Thought Worthy Of Love

You see, beloved, how great and wonderful a thing is love, and that there is no declaring its perfection. Who is fit to be found in it, except such as God has vouchsafed to render so? Let us pray, therefore, and implore of His mercy, that we may live blameless in love, free from all human partialities for one above another. All the generations from Adam even unto this day have passed away; but those who, through the grace of God, have been made perfect in love, now possess a place among the godly, and shall be made manifest at the revelation[1] of the kingdom of Christ. For it is written, "Enter into thy secret chambers for a little time, until my wrath and fury pass away; and I will remember a propitious[2] day, and will raise you up out of your graves."[3] Blessed are we, beloved, if we keep the commandments of God in the harmony of love; that so through love our sins may be forgiven us. For it is written, "Blessed are they whose transgressions are forgiven, and whose sins are covered. Blessed is the man whose sin the Lord will not impute to him, and in whose mouth there is no guile."[4] This blessedness cometh upon those who have been chosen by God through Jesus Christ our Lord; to whom be glory for ever and ever. Amen.

---

1. Literally, "visitation."
2. Or, "good."
3. Isa. 26:20.
4. Ps. 32:1-2.

CHAPTER LI

Let The Partakers In Strife Acknowledge Their Sins

LET US THEREFORE implore forgiveness for all those transgressions which through any [suggestion] of the adversary we have committed. And those who have been the leaders of sedition and disagreement ought to have respect[1] to the common hope. For such as live in fear and love would rather that they themselves than their neighbours should be involved in suffering. And they prefer to bear blame themselves, rather than that the concord which has been well and piously[2] handed down to us should suffer. For it is better that a man should acknowledge his transgressions than that he should harden his heart, as the hearts of those were hardened who stirred up sedition against Moses the servant of God, and whose condemnation was made manifest [unto all]. For they went down alive into Hades, and death swallowed them up.[3] Pharaoh with his army and all the princes of Egypt, and the chariots with their riders, were sunk in the depths of the Red Sea, and perished,[4] for no other reason than that their foolish hearts were hardened, after so many signs and wonders had been wrought in the land of Egypt by Moses the servant of God.

---

1. Or, "look to."
2. Or, "righteously."
3. Num. 16.
4. Ex. 14.

CHAPTER LII

Such A Confession Is Pleasing To God

THE LORD, BRETHREN, stands in need of nothing; and He desires nothing of anyone, except that confession be made to Him. For, says the elect David, "I will confess unto the Lord; and that will please Him more than a young bullock that hath horns and hoofs. Let the poor see it, and be glad."[1] And again he saith, "Offer[2] unto God the sacrifice of praise, and pay thy vows unto the Most High. And call upon Me in the day of thy trouble: I will deliver thee, and thou shalt glorify Me.[3] For the sacrifice of God is a broken spirit."[4]

---

1. Ps. 69:31-32.
2. Or, "sacrifice."
3. Ps. 50:14-15.
4. Ps. 51:17.

CHAPTER LIII

The Love Of Moses Towards His People

You understand, beloved, you understand well the Sacred Scriptures, and you have looked very earnestly into the oracles of God. Call then these things to your remembrance. When Moses went up into the mount, and abode there, with fasting and humiliation, forty days and forty nights, the Lord said unto him, "Moses, Moses, get thee down quickly from hence; for thy people whom thou didst bring out of the land of Egypt have committed iniquity. They have speedily departed from the way in which I commanded them to walk, and have made to themselves molten images."[1] And the Lord said unto him, "I have spoken to thee once and again, saying, I have seen this people, and, behold, it is a stiff-necked people: let Me destroy them, and blot out their name from under heaven; and I will make thee a great and wonderful nation, and one much more numerous than this."[2] But Moses said, "Far be it from Thee, Lord: pardon the sin of this people; else blot me also out of the book of the living."[3] O marvelous[4] love! O insuperable perfection! The servant speaks freely to his Lord, and asks forgiveness for the people, or begs that he himself might perish[5] along with them.

---

1. Ex. 32:7, etc.; Deut. 9:12, etc.
2. Ex. 32:9, etc.
3. Ex. 32:32.
4. Or, "mighty."
5. Literally, "be wiped out."

CHAPTER LIV

He Who Is Full Of Love Will Incur Every Loss, That Peace May Be Restored To The Church

WHO THEN AMONG you is noble-minded? Who compassionate? Who full of love? Let him declare, "If on my account sedition and disagreement and schisms have arisen, I will depart, I will go away whithersoever you desire, and I will do whatever the majority[1] commands; only let the flock of Christ live on terms of peace with the presbyters set over it." He that acts thus shall procure to himself great glory in the Lord; and every place will welcome[2] him. For "the earth is the Lord›s, and the fulness thereof."[3] These things they who live a godly life, that is never to be repented of, both have done and always will do.

---

1. Literally, "the multitude." [Clement here puts words into the mouth of the Corinthian presbyters. It has been strangely quoted to strengthen a conjecture that he had humbly preferred Linus and Cletus when first called to preside.]
2. Or, "receive."
3. Ps. 24:1; 1 Cor. 10:26, 28.

CHAPTER LV

Examples Of Such Love

To BRING FORWARD some examples from among the heathen: Many kings and princes, in times of pestilence, when they had been instructed by an oracle, have given themselves up to death, in order that by their own blood they might deliver their fellow-citizens [from destruction]. Many have gone forth from their own cities, that so sedition might be brought to an end within them. We know many among ourselves who have given themselves up to bonds, in order that they might ransom others. Many, too, have surrendered themselves to slavery, that with the price[1] which they received for themselves, they might provide food for others. Many women also, being strengthened by the grace of God, have performed numerous manly exploits. The blessed Judith, when her city was besieged, asked of the elders permission to go forth into the camp of the strangers; and, exposing herself to danger, she went out for the love which she bare to her country and people then besieged; and the Lord delivered Holofernes into the hands of a woman.[2] Esther also, being perfect in faith, exposed herself to no less danger, in order to deliver the twelve tribes of Israel from impending destruction. For with fasting and humiliation she entreated the everlasting God, who seeth all things; and He, perceiving the humility of her spirit, delivered the people for whose sake she had encountered peril.[3]

---

1. Literally, "and having received their prices, fed others." [Comp. Rom. xvi. 3, 4, and Phil. ii. 30.]
2. Judith 8:30.
3. Esth. 7, 8.

CHAPTER LVI

Let Us Admonish And Correct One Another

Let us then also pray for those who have fallen into any sin, that meekness and humility may be given to them, so that they may submit, not unto us, but to the will of God. For in this way they shall secure a fruitful and perfect remembrance from us, with sympathy for them, both in our prayers to God, and our mention of them to the saints.[1] Let us receive correction, beloved, on account of which no one should feel displeased. Those exhortations by which we admonish one another are both good [in themselves] and highly profitable, for they tend to unite[2] us to the will of God. For thus saith the holy Word: "The Lord hath severely chastened me, yet hath not given me over to death."[3] "For whom the Lord loveth He chasteneth, and scourgeth every son whom He receiveth."[4] "The righteous," saith it, "shall chasten me in mercy, and reprove me; but let not the oil of sinners make fat my head."[5] And again he saith,

> Blessed is the man whom the Lord reproveth, and reject not thou the warning of the Almighty. For He causes sorrow, and again restores [to gladness]; He woundeth, and His hands make whole. He shall deliver thee in six troubles, yea, in the seventh no evil shall touch thee. In famine He shall rescue thee from death, and in war

---

1. Literally, "there shall be to them a fruitful and perfect remembrance, with compassions both towards God and the saints."
2. Or, "they unite."
3. Ps. 118:18.
4. Prov. 3:12; Heb. 12:6.
5. Ps. 141:5.

He shall free thee from the power[6] of the sword. From the scourge of the tongue will He hide thee, and thou shalt not fear when evil cometh. Thou shalt laugh at the unrighteous and the wicked, and shalt not be afraid of the beasts of the field. For the wild beasts shall be at peace with thee: then shalt thou know that thy house shall be in peace, and the habitation of thy tabernacle shall not fail.[7] Thou shall know also that thy seed shall be great, and thy children like the grass of the field. And thou shall come to the grave like ripened corn which is reaped in its season, or like a heap of the threshing-floor which is gathered together at the proper time."[8]

You see, beloved, that protection is afforded to those that are chastened of the Lord; for since God is good, He corrects us, that we may be admonished by His holy chastisement.

---

6. Literally, "hand."
7. Literally, "err" or "sin."
8. Job 5:17-26.

CHAPTER LVII

Let The Authors Of Sedition Submit Themselves

YOU THEREFORE, who laid the foundation of this sedition, submit yourselves to the presbyters, and receive correction so as to repent, bending the knees of your hearts. Learn to be subject, laying aside the proud and arrogant self-confidence of your tongue. For it is better for you that you should occupy[1] a humble but honourable place in the flock of Christ, than that, being highly exalted, you should be cast out from the hope of His people.[2] For thus speaketh all-virtuous Wisdom:[3] "Behold, I will bring forth to you the words of My Spirit, and I will teach you My speech. Since I called, and you did not hear; I held forth My words, and you regarded not, but set at naught My counsels, and yielded not at My reproofs; therefore I too will laugh at your destruction; yea, I will rejoice when ruin cometh upon you, and when sudden confusion overtakes you, when overturning presents itself like a tempest, or when tribulation and oppression fall upon you. For it shall come to pass, that when you call upon Me, I will not hear you; the wicked shall seek Me, and they shall not find Me. For they hated wisdom, and did not choose the fear of the Lord; nor would they listen to My counsels, but despised My reproofs. Wherefore they shall eat the fruits of their own way, and they shall be filled with

---

1. Literally, "to be found small and esteemed."
2. Literally, "His hope." [It has been conjectured that ἔλπιδος should be ἐπαύλιδος, and the reading, "out of the fold of his people." See Chevallier.]
3. Prov. 1:23-31. [Often cited by this name in primitive writers.]

their own ungodliness." ...[4]

---

4. Junius (Pat. Young), who examined the ms. before it was bound into its present form, stated that a whole leaf was here lost. The next letters that occur are ιπον, which have been supposed to indicate εἶπον or ἔλιπον. Doubtless some passages quoted by the ancients from the Epistle of Clement, and not now found in it, occurred in the portion which has thus been lost.

CHAPTER LVIII

Blessings Sought For All That Call Upon God

MAY GOD, who seeth all things, and who is the Ruler of all spirits and the Lord of all flesh – who chose our Lord Jesus Christ and us through Him to be a peculiar[1] people – grant to every soul that calleth upon His glorious and holy Name, faith, fear, peace, patience, long-suffering, self-control, purity, and sobriety, to the well-pleasing of His Name, through our High Priest and Protector, Jesus Christ, by whom be to Him glory, and majesty, and power, and honour, both now and for evermore. Amen.

---

1. Comp. Tit. 2:14.

CHAPTER LIX

The Corinthians Are Exhorted Speedily To Send Back Word That Peace Has Been Restored: The Benediction

SEND BACK SPEEDILY to us in peace and with joy these our messengers to you: Claudius Ephebus and Valerius Bito, with Fortunatus: that they may the sooner announce to us the peace and harmony we so earnestly desire and long for [among you], and that we may the more quickly rejoice over the good order re-established among you. The grace of our Lord Jesus Christ be with you, and with all everywhere that are the called of God through Him, by whom be to Him glory, honour, power, majesty, and eternal dominion,[1] from everlasting to everlasting.[2] Amen.[3]

---

1. Literally, "an eternal throne."
2. Literally, "From the ages to the ages of ages."
3. [Note St. Clement's frequent doxologies.] [N.B.—The language of Clement concerning the Western progress of St. Paul (cap. v.) is our earliest postscript to his Scripture biography. It is sufficient to refer the reader to the great works of Conybeare and Howson, and of Mr. Lewin, on the *Life and Epistles of St. Paul*. See more especially the valuable note of Lewin (vol. ii. p. 294) which takes notice of the opinion of some learned men, that the great Apostle of the Gentiles preached the Gospel in Britain. The whole subject of St. Paul's relations with British Christians is treated by Williams, in his *Antiquities of the Cymry*, with learning and in an attractive manner. But the reader will find more ready to his hand, perhaps, the interesting note of Mr. Lewin, on Claudia and Pudens (2 Tim. 4:21), in his *Life and Epistles of St. Paul*, vol. ii. p. 392. See also Paley's *Horæ Paulinæ*, p. 40. London, 1820.]

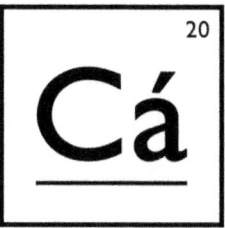

About the Cántaro Institute
Inheriting, Informing, Inspiring

The Cántaro Institute is a reformed evangelical Christian organization committed to the advancement of the Christian worldview for the reformation and renewal of the church and culture.

We believe that as the Christian church returns to the fount of Scripture as her ultimate authority for all knowing and living, and wisely applies God's truth to every aspect of life, her missiological activity will result in not only the renewal of the human person but also the reformation of culture, an inevitable result when the true scope and nature of the gospel is made known and applied.